The Hollows of Bone

poems by

Isabella J. Mansfield

Finishing Line Press
Georgetown, Kentucky

The Hollows of Bone

Copyright © 2019 by Isabella J. Mansfield
ISBN 978-1-63534-817-0 First Edition
All rights reserved under International and Pan-American Copyright Conventions. No part of this book may be reproduced in any manner whatsoever without written permission from the publisher, except in the case of brief quotations embodied in critical articles and reviews.

ACKNOWLEDGMENTS

2018 Mark Ritzenhein New Author Award Winner

"Aisle 9…" was a Semi-Finalist for the 2017 Brittany Noakes Award

"My Naked Body," "Local Woman Accidentally Terrorizes…," "Climate Change," were featured by Philosophical Idiot philosophicalidiot.com

Publisher: Leah Maines
Editor: Christen Kincaid
Cover Art and Design: Alison Baionno, Instagram @ali.delphia
Author Photo: Linda Michele-Dobel, lmd-photography.com

Printed in the USA on acid-free paper.
Order online: www.finishinglinepress.com
also available on amazon.com

Author inquiries and mail orders:
Finishing Line Press
P. O. Box 1626
Georgetown, Kentucky 40324
U. S. A.

Table of Contents

Untitled Poem About Apathy 1
…And They Said Fresh Air Would Be Good for Me 2
Wide W Strokes 3
I Don't Write Nature Poetry 4
Climate Change 5
She 6
Burnt 7
#momlife 8
Wound Up 9
The Emergency Department Is Freezing 10
Breaking Point 12
Old Man 13
(untitled haiku) 15
Crisis Point 16
Bruises 17
My Naked Body 18
I Am (a series of senryu) 19
Wrong 20
They Run Lines 21
She Is A Gray Area 22
Cattails In Ice 23
(untitled senryu) 24
"Local Woman Accidentally Terrorizes Target Customers
    With Noisy, Clearance Halloween Décor That Won't
    Turn Off." 25
Writemares 28
To the Girl Giving Head in the Back of the Parking Lot 29
Aisle Nine: Bottled Water, Juice, Clearance, Bible Verses,
    Unwanted Attention 30

*For the people in my life who worry about me sometimes, thanks.
I'm okay.
For my BFFs—you know who you are.
For the many writers I have come to know all over the world, thank
you for always being a source of guidance, inspiration and
countless inappropriate jokes.*

Untitled Poem About Apathy

apathy is supposed to be about not feeling
but what i feel is hands around a heart
a tightened grip and then . . .
a hyper-awareness of the empty space
where feelings should go
where feelings used to go
but were mislabeled, then lost
placed in a box marked "garbage"
instead of a box marked "important"
or filed alphabetically and saved for later
maybe "love" got mixed up with "loneliness"
or a clerical error confused "validation" with "void"
and "empathy" with "empty"

apathy feels like failure
when it hurts—
it isn't supposed to hurt—
maybe the pain is proof
that the heart still beats
but I didn't ask for proof
or proof of purchase
I do not need a receipt for my anxiety
this is final sale, there are no exchanges, no returns
you cannot return from this place
once it has that grip around your heart

apathy is a vast, gaping canyon
greater than grand,
a snapshot
in grainy black and white
missing the nuances of sky and cloud
and rock, of sunset on trees
it is the tree, barren and twisted,
reaching for a light that keeps
moving away from gnarled fingers
but not caring when it slips
away into a bleak, star-filled night

...And They Said Fresh Air Would Be Good for Me

I pulled at stubborn weeds,
bare fingers in the dirt.
It wasn't warm enough for this,
my hands, cold and stained brown,
displaced earth and sleepy worms,
grabbed at unfamiliar shoots.
I thought about your suicide,
your destruction,
and what it would mean
if we, too, were pulled
by the root and discarded.

Wide W Strokes

you can almost hear
the paint roller, can't you?
It makes a sickening,
sticking sound,
up and down,
depositing a dark
enough blue
to cover years of
deep red neglect.

I Don't Write Nature Poetry

Nature is a dense fog—
low and heavy for you
to hide in

Nature is a river
to carry you downstream
when hiding isn't enough

Nature is the ocean that receives you,
crushing depths and suffocating
under immense pressure

Nature is sunsets
and every day the sun
abandons you

Nature is an apologetic sunrise
you know will leave you
again and again

Nature is a full moon—
clear and bright
but so lonely

Nature is flowers
ripped up at their peak
left to brown and die

Climate Change

nobody
ever told me
that apathy
is more damaging
than acid rain
and hurts worse
but only
for a little while

She

She is in danger.

She is broken, exhausted, feels unloved and she is in danger.

She is at risk of abducting herself from a life that seems to not want her. She walks railroad tracks and roads in the dark and waits for danger around the corner.

She is dry tinder in a house made of matchsticks, of flint. She will catch fire and burn out. She has already burned out. She will reignite and burn out again.

She loves hard and gives all, leaves nothing for herself. She has tried to fix this, has forced herself to be independent— guilt tugs her back. She feels alone and feels bad about that because she's not alone. She is sorry for leaving you alone so she can be alone. She is aware of the contradiction. She is sorry about that too; she knows nothing makes sense anymore.

She has one foot on the starting line and the other on a cliff. She waits for the gun to startle her in either direction. She is ready to run or to jump. She does not care which.

She is in danger. She feels wings grow back where they were clipped. She is itching to stretch a full wingspan, see if she remembers how to fly. She is afraid to fly.

She needs simultaneously to be loved and held close and left alone. She is unsure of how to act anymore. She is forgetting how to love. She does not want to leave, but does not know how to stay.

She wants you to know she takes the blame for all of it, for every hurt you feel and the hurt she feels. She knows.

She is the danger.

Burnt

I
am
exhausted
from
holding
everything
up
and
there
is
nothing
left
to
hold
me

#momlife

There are little hands

pounding

on my bedroom door,
my bathroom door left slightly ajar
my shower door closed to keep the water in
there are little hands

pounding

on my bedroom door
I pretend I can't hear it, immersing
my face into streams of water
turning the dial up
a volume set to "hotter still"
bristling, a bit too hot but not adjusting back
letting lava pour over my scalp,
my reddened skin, silencing the

pounding

at the door, at my temples
for a blissful six minutes
of almost-alone

Wound Up

the muscles
in my thighs
are twitching

in my
shoulders
there are knots

in my side
a little key
and every minute

it gets turned
tighter still —
I can feel

the spring
winding
below my

ribcage
the gear
scraping

against bone
the coil
wrapping

under skin
the metal
yielding

giving way
but not
without

permanent
strain
and damage

The Emergency Department Is Freezing

I should have expected this,
it is the same in every hospital,
but I am in shorts and a tee-shirt
because you never expect to be
in the emergency room.

We are supposed to be at lunch;
filling our empty bellies
might have made you feel better.
Dinner will be late tonight
and I feel the ache of skipping breakfast.
Hindsight is 20/20,
and hungry, too.

In your hospital gown, you look small,
not like my mother.
You apologize
for the inconvenience,
for the trouble,
wanting to go home,
while we wait for the all clear
to walk out the door.

It was my mother who smoothed the rough roads
so seamlessly. Most days I don't realize that now,
on the other side of mid-thirties,
I, too, have joined the ranks of adulthood.

It is me now, sitting at a hospital bedside,
where she sat so often for me.
She carried strength and grace in her arms,
kept worry and fear in her pocket
and out of sight.

It is me now, watching her wait,
watching worried lines dance on her face,
her face that is my face—
my brown eyes and my nose.

It is me now, holding court at her side,
a jester, pulling strings
to raise the corners of her mouth,
to distract and put at ease.

It is me now, keeping worry and fear in my pocket,
and out of sight.

Breaking Point

I sat tonight on my filthy kitchen floor
and sobbed
into a red bandana.

My five-year-old, screaming in his room,
stopped suddenly
in apparent alarm.

This noise coming from the kitchen
from his mother, this noise
he had never heard before.

"STOP!" he shouted,
marching in, still in his school uniform
smelling of goldfish crackers.

"STOP" he shouted, over and over
to my tear-streaked face,
before twisting and contorting his own.

Then, we cried together on the dirty floor
with our backs
against the dishwasher.

Old Man

My dad got lost four times
on the way to my place:
twice on the straightaway
and once on my own street,
despite clear directions
and just how many stop signs.
I don't know how to spend a week with him
after that, when I don't know what else to say
knowing he only half-listens
and the other half doesn't hear
(No longer just the tinnitus
that has plagued him since his twenties.)
I don't know how to watch the man
Responsible for half of my DNA
…Slip away…

I used to feel the stubble on his cheeks
and draw stick figures with bushy mustaches and glasses
next to shorter sticks wearing triangle dresses.
The mustache is gone, his stubble is white.
(It still looks just as prickly.)
We used to sing together or feed the squirrels.
As a girl he'd take me fishing, skating, shopping.
My interests changed, but he was there.
I was one of the lucky ones:
My friends had dads of the deadbeat variety,
but mine made the effort no matter the distance.
He still tells me I can do anything. (I can.)
And I used to think that he could, too. (He can't.)
He moves slow, an old man version of my dad.
He tells me he still smokes too much,
but his other vices are under control

("Mostly," he says, referring to the booze
he knows I worry about but don't know how to ask.)

I see my grandfather in him now:
in those last years my dad described his father
as "sharp as a tack,"
though the doctors usually spelled it "dementia."

(untitled haiku)

water on a rock
continually pounding
nothing left but sand

Crisis Point

my favorite shirt hangs
my new jeans slip from hips
bones protrude at my wrist
   at my shoulders
   at my back
bruises cure in yellow-purple patches
and yet—
all they say is how great!
   how hard I've worked!
   how it paid off!
how I'm stronger!
       faster!
       better!

but I don't see it
       and they don't know how I feel
       and I don't know how I feel
       and I can't make it stop

I wonder if eventually
I will disappear
and when the wind fills the empty spaces
       the hollows of bone
you will hear them rattle:
"She's never looked better."

Bruises

I bruise easier than before.

I don't notice them:
they don't hurt unless
I push them
which I only do
when they're first discovered—
that unconscious need
to touch
the thing that hurts.

My Naked Body

my naked body
is a work of art

I don't know
if the artist was

Rubens or Dali
or Picasso

I am trying
to find beauty

in it but isn't all
art subjective?

I Am (a series of senryu)

I am loose skin on
bones that ache and muscles that
bruise too easily

I am soft sighs and
hard swallows not unnoticed
but not tended to

I am pressure on
forehead, across furrowed brows
but genuine smiles

I am syllables
counted out on my fingers
writing every word

I am not something
to be devoured, to be
wanted, but I want

I am trying to
be everything you need and
I'm not succeeding

I am trying to
remember who I am with—
maybe without you

Wrong

my body is wrong
my hips are wrong
my legs are wrong
my stomach is wrong
my tits are wrong
my body is *wrong*
nothing works the way it should
the way they say
nothing looks the way they say
it should
and they tell you "maybe one day"
"maybe if you looked like this"
but they never tell you
how to fix it, just that it is wrong
and they never show you theirs
but they tell you yours is wrong
but you can't let them know
they got to you because they're sensitive
and they'll call you "too sensitive"
and you think "maybe ten more pounds"
after the fifty you've already lost
and you wonder how much work
to burn off that bite
and you push harder
cut your slice smaller
smaller still
and you say you're not tired
not hungry
but you're wrong

They Run Lines

blue ones in my arms
connect to clear ones
taped down
plastic snakes
that drip
slow
  legal
    venom

She Is a Gray Area

she is a gray area.
gaunt,
and thin
in her heart;
apathy now
the only thing
that fits her well
and she wears it
under everything
every day.

Cattails In Ice

pavement curves
    snakes around lakes
      only cattails edge the road
    stiff and shimmering
       wafer thin ice
frost at the top
  guardrails won't stop
    my nightmare where the water
                covers the road, plunging me below
  the surface and I claw at water
at my chest
  as if that will let
        the air into my lungs

(untitled senryu)

I am already
at war with myself, don't you
start firing, too

"Local Woman Accidentally Terrorizes Target Customers with Noisy Clearance Halloween Decor That Won't Turn Off."

I thought to myself as I stood in the store
manager's office, "I don't know how I got here,
how it escalated to this."

Minding my own business, like every other
suburban mom, meandering every red and white
aisle with a burnt cup of coffee, a

nagging forgetfulness for the one thing
I needed and will again leave without
(dishwasher soap, if you're keeping track)

and lured to the back of the store by
yellow and black tags screaming
"Seventy percent off!"

Pumpkin.
Spice.
Everything.

And covered in glitter, crows covered in glitter,
headstones covered in glitter, bones
covered in glitter and broken

chipped plastic skulls staring in packs of
pink and green and marigold,
Dia de los Desecration. . .

But crushed velvet pumpkins!
and candlesticks! and skeletons! and spiders!
and things that go bump! and there:

there in the aisle between
Halloween and Christmas,
the vintage gothic

telephone with the fake rotary dial,
paramount style, a handset I'll have
to explain to my son how to hold,

and the booming, creepy voice, 70% off,
nestled into my cart between discount candy
I don't need, foam pumpkins and the

space for the dishwasher soap
I still haven't remembered. Twenty people,
maybe more, before the exit. It began.

"I'M COMING FOR YOU"

In the cereal aisle, the nice young couple and the alarmed baby

"HOW DARE YOU"

To the soup, the man buying Spaghettios

"LOOK BEHIND YOU"

the woman at the peanut butter, only she turned around and said "geez, lady"

I moved quick through the aisles but only
egged it on, motion sensors fired faster,
dread filled me at every turn

"I KNOW WHO YOU ARE"

Evil laughter rang through the store. From aisles down,
shoppers looked at me in shock,
as though I was the threat.

"COME WITH ME TO THE GRAVE"

And before I could remember the dishwasher soap,
before I reached the greeting
cards, it haunted, taunted

Every customer it passed. Every child.
Every red shirt and khaki pants...except one.
"Ma'am..." said the manager.

"All I wanted was a pumpkin!"
In retrospect... I probably shouldn't
have shouted.

I thought to myself as I stood in the store
manager's office, "I don't know how
I got here, how it escalated to this."

"All I wanted was a pumpkin."

Writemares

looking down the barrel of a mic
white hot light
pale in the bright
trying to remember how to
breathe
how to read and second guessing
every line I've ever written

if it looks effortless
I am a better actor than poet
a master of disguise
hide my hands beneath my thighs
stop my feet from tapping
Morse Code spelling out "SHE IS A FRAUD!
AFRAID! You can see it in her eyes"

these are lies
every letter my mouth forms
any heart my word warms
they are false
and I tremble in these writemares
these stage frightmares
knowing I will be seen
knowing this is no dream

knowing I will come back for more
a monthly encore
sneaking out the stage door,
—shake more—
this spoken word
this need to be heard
is harder than it seems
even harder than the dreams

To the Girl Giving Head in the Back of the Parking Lot

We see you.

You'd think we wouldn't with the covert way your cars are parked so close together; with the way two adults are casually seated in the back of a midsize sedan at the back of a Kohl's parking lot at 7pm on a Tuesday, but the summer sun doesn't set for three more hours...

and we see you...

but we're not judging you, because if we're honest, sometimes you just need to get away for a little while and babysitters are expensive. Sometimes you just need to go away—pretend your life isn't spiraling out of control. The sedan doesn't need an oil change and a detail as badly as the minivan, plus: it has a bench seat in the back, instead of captains chairs cradling car seats, cup holders concealing goldfish crackers, and wrappers from the Snickers bar you ate at the red light or the Starbucks cup you mostly emptied on the way to carpool and the envelope full of grocery coupons you always forget to use.

The sedan is just generally cleaner without kids, as most things usually are, and the bench seat is comfortable and quiet and the two of you can sit and pretend that this is normal, that you're "just talking" in the back where you can sit next to each other, your feet momentarily in his lap.

We see you; that you both struggle to relax, even on a comfortable bench seat, with the air blowing just as hard as you are, because the risk is high but you can pretend you're seventeen again and isn't the risk half of the fun? Tinted windows were a nice upgrade, but silhouettes are still noticeable when one is constantly looking around and the other suddenly disappears.

We see you...but we're not judging you, because sometimes we're all the girl in the back of the parking lot, even if only in our imaginations, and later, when the minivan is parked in the garage and the sedan pulls up with a pizza to share, and you two exchange a knowing glance, we won't have room to judge, because we will wish we had something as strong as you and your parking lot secret.

Aisle Nine: Bottled Water, Juice, Clearance, Bible Verses, Unwanted Attention

A man prayed over me in the clearance aisle
of our neighborhood grocery store—
for my healing
for the health of my broken body.
He called me "sister," said it wasn't enough
to just say the words.
"You have to give them power;
you have to feel it."

I couldn't tell him that people have laid their hands
on me in every grocery store from here to Arizona
for the last 25 years and all it ever did
was make me late or melt the ice cream.

I couldn't tell him a miracle would be nice
but I'm not holding my breath
for the days he'll see me turn cartwheels
down that very aisle.

I couldn't tell him how I'm in the middle
of a crisis of faith, however unrelated
to my "condition,"
how I feel empty inside
a crowded church,
how I should be bothered by this,
but I'm not
because you can't miss something
if you aren't really sure
it was ever there.

Isabella J. Mansfield listens almost exclusively to the same seven albums from 1994. She loves coffee, movies, sarcasm, and is occasionally prone to exaggeration. Writing mostly free-verse poetry about lust, anxiety, and the human condition, she enjoys senryu and tanka, but otherwise ignores traditional "rules" when it comes to writing.

Author of two self-published chapbooks, Mansfield's poetry has been featured by *Philosophical Idiot, The Weekly Avocet, The Reverie Journal* and *The Prose Haiku Edition*. In 2017, she was selected as a Semi-Finalist for the Second Annual Brittany Noakes Award. In 2018, she received the Mark Ritzenhein New Author Award. She lives in Howell, Michigan, with her husband and son.

www.ingramcontent.com/pod-product-compliance
Lightning Source LLC
LaVergne TN
LVHW041509070426
835507LV00012B/1434